Made in United States
Troutdale, OR
07/16/2025

32958307R00064